Searchlight BOOKS™

Celebrating Failure

Great

Invention Fails

Barbara Krasner

Lerner Publications ◆ Minneapolis

Lerner Publications Company
An imprint of Lerner Publishing Group, Inc.
241 First Avenue North
Minneapolis, MN 55401 USA

For reading levels and more information, look up this title at www.lernerbooks.com.

Main body text set in Adrianna Regular.
Typeface provided by Chank.

Library of Congress Cataloging-in-Publication Data

Title: Great invention fails / Barbara Krasner.
Description: Minneapolis : Lerner Publications, [2020] | Series: Searchlight books.
    Celebrating failure | Audience: Ages 8–11. | Audience: Grades 4 to 6.
Identifiers: LCCN 2019013428 (print) | LCCN 2019019822 (ebook) |
    ISBN 9781541583375 (eb pdf) | ISBN 9781541577336 (lb : alk. paper)
Subjects: LCSH: Inventions—History—Juvenile literature. | Inventors—Juvenile literature.
Classification: LCC T48 (ebook) | LCC T48 .K73 2020 (print) | DDC 609—dc23

LC record available at https://lccn.loc.gov/2019013428

Manufactured in the United States of America
1-46755-47746-6/6/2019

Contents

Chapter 1

BUBBLE TROUBLE

Ordinary wallpaper is flat, just like a sheet of paper. In 1957 American engineer Alfred Fielding and Swiss chemist Marc Chavannes had a new idea. They wanted to make textured wallpaper. Using heat, they joined two plastic shower curtains together. To make a texture, they left some air bubbles between the curtains. But customers did not like their bubbly plastic wallpaper.

The inventors of Bubble Wrap started out making wallpaper. That idea failed.

The Bubble Wrap inventors eventually realized that their creation would make great packing material.

Fielding and Chavannes did not give up on their invention. Maybe their bubble-filled plastic could line the glass walls of greenhouses. That would help warm the plants there. That idea didn't take off either.

Fielding and Chavannes still didn't give up. They decided their invention would make good packaging material. They called it Bubble Wrap.

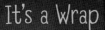
It's a Wrap

Before the invention of Bubble Wrap, most companies wadded up old newspapers and packed them around products for shipping. But ink from the newspapers sometimes made products dirty.

Bubble Wrap is better than wadded-up newspaper because it's cleaner and more cushiony.

IN THE 1960s, IBM WRAPPED ITS BIG COMPUTERS IN BUBBLE WRAP FOR SHIPMENT.

Bubble Wrap was a better option. It was clean, and its cushiony air bubbles kept products from breaking during shipment. Computer maker IBM and other big companies began packing products in Bubble Wrap.

A Sealed Air worker moves rolls of Bubble Wrap at the company's plant in New Jersey.

Soon Fielding and Chavannes produced many different kinds of Bubble Wrap, with air bubbles of different sizes, shapes, and strengths. Their company, Sealed Air, became a big success. By 2017, it had fifteen thousand employees. It sells Bubble Wrap and other packing materials to customers around the world.

Failure Leads to Success

Like Alfred Fielding and Marc Chavannes, many inventors fail again and again. Some of them give up. But others refuse to let failure stand in their way. In fact, some of the greatest inventions of all time began as failures.

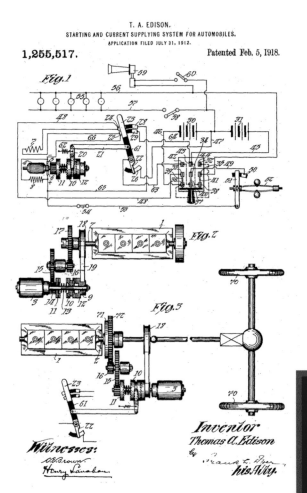

T. A. EDISON.
STARTING AND CURRENT SUPPLYING SYSTEM FOR AUTOMOBILES.
APPLICATION FILED JULY 31, 1912.

1,255,517.

Patented Feb. 5, 1918.

Inventor Thomas Edison designed a charging system for cars in the early twentieth century and filed his design with the US Patent Office.

The Road to Failure

In the 1950s and 1960s, three-dimensional (3D) movies were popular. They looked lifelike. The 1960 movie *Scent of Mystery* was supposed to be lifelike too. The theaters that showed it installed Smell-O-Vision. This system, created by Swiss inventor Hans Laube, sent different odors drifting through theaters. For instance, when the movie showed the seashore, moviegoers smelled a salty ocean breeze.

But sometimes the smells arrived too late or reached only parts of the theater. Audiences didn't like Smell-O-Vision. Laube's invention was a failure. But people loved 3D movies. They are still popular in the twenty-first century.

An advertisement for *Scent of Mystery*

Chapter 2

STICKY BUSINESS

In 1968, chemist Spencer Silver worked at 3M in Minnesota. The company made many products, such as tape, sandpaper, and glue. Silver was trying to create a strong glue for building airplanes.

This photo from about 1960 shows an aerial view of 3M in Maplewood, Minnesota.

Can you guess what new product Silver's not-so-sticky glue led to?

Silver did create a new type of glue, but it wasn't very strong. It was only sticky enough to hold two pieces of paper together. Someone could easily pull the pieces of paper apart again. The managers at 3M wanted a strong glue, not a weak one. So Silver's

A Better Bookmark

Another 3M scientist, Arthur Fry, sang in a church choir. He used paper bookmarks to keep track of pages in his

songbook. But they often fell out onto the floor. In 1974, Fry remembered Spencer Silver's glue.

Arthur Fry, shown here in the twenty-first century, helped turn Spencer Silver's failed glue into a successful product.

Back at the lab at 3M, Fry applied the glue to the back of a paper bookmark. Because the glue was so weak, he could put the marker on one page of a book, pull it off again, and then move it to another page of the book. The glue didn't leave a sticky film on the pages.

Before Silver invented his glue, there was no such thing as glue that didn't leave a sticky residue behind.

late!!!

At first, no one wanted
Silver's weak glue. But
the glue was perfect for
making sticky notes.

Fry and Silver worked together to turn their idea into
a new product. Their sticky papers were more than just
bookmarks. People could write notes on the front and
stick the papers onto desks, business letters, and even
coffee cups—anywhere someone wanted to leave a note.

POST-IT NOTES ARE A BIG MONEYMAKER FOR THE 3M COMPANY.

The managers at 3M liked the papers too. They named them Post-it Notes. Soon 3M was selling Post-it Notes in many different colors, sizes, and styles. Spencer Silver's glue was not a failure after all. It was a smashing success. In the twenty-first century, 3M sells more than fifty billion Post-it Notes per year.

Failing Upward

In 1908 famous US inventor Thomas Edison (*below*) designed a concrete house. Unlike wooden houses, concrete houses won't burn down in a fire. Edison also wanted to make concrete furniture to go inside his concrete houses.

But concrete houses were expensive and hard to build. His idea never took off.

More than one hundred years later, Edison's idea is back. Building with concrete is easier and cheaper than it used to be. Some builders want to fight homelessness with 3D-printed concrete houses. The houses would protect people from fire, hurricanes, and other dangers. Edison's old failure might be a success after all.

Chapter 3

DYE JOB

In 1856, William Perkin was a student at the Royal College of Chemistry in London. His professor gave him an assignment: Create a synthetic version of quinine, a drug for malaria. Perkin mixed coal tar and other chemicals in a glass beaker to make quinine. But all he got was a dark sludge.

William Perkin studied at the Royal College of Chemistry. He tried to make quinine in the laboratory, but he didn't succeed.

When Perkin tried to wash out the beaker with alcohol, the sludge turned a bright shade of purple. When Perkin wiped the purple sludge with cloth, the cloth turned purple too. Perkin knew he had invented something important: the first synthetic dye.

William Perkin, shown here with his wife, accidentally invented a purple dye.

IN EARLIER CENTURIES, PEOPLE USED MUREX, A KIND OF SHELLFISH, TO MAKE PURPLE DYE.

Before Perkin's invention, people made dyes from natural materials, such as flowers, berries, and even the bodies of insects. One purple dye, called Tyrian purple, came from the murex, a type of shellfish. Making natural dyes was time-consuming and expensive. The colors were dull and often faded over time.

The Color Purple

But Perkin's purple dye was different. It was easy to make in the lab. The color was brilliant, and clothing dyed with synthetic dye did not fade after washing. Perkin named the color mauveine, or mauve, after a purple flower.

Perkin named his dye after a pretty purple flower.

This dress from the turn of the last century was dyed purple with Perkin's dye.

In Paris and London, people loved Perkin's purple dye. Girls wore mauve ribbons in their hair. Britain's Queen Victoria wore a mauve gown to her daughter's wedding.

Perkin convinced his family to invest in the dye business. They produced synthetic dyes in many colors. William Perkin had failed to make a drug to treat malaria, but his failure kicked off a brand-new industry.

William Perkin failed to make quinine but launched the synthetic dye industry instead.

Chapter 4

THE CAR OF TOMORROW

In 1933, American inventor Buckminster Fuller designed the Dymaxion car. This big, blimp-shaped car had room for eleven passengers. It had two wheels in front and one in back. Fuller was excited about this car. He said it would speed along at 90 miles (145 km) an hour. He said it would handle the roughest roads.

Buckminster Fuller designed many vehicles and structures. Here he shows a model of his Dymaxion house.

Most exciting of all, Fuller said that in the future, the car would fly. At this time, jet airplanes hadn't been invented. Neither had helicopters. But Fuller said that when that technology was ready, his car would take off like a helicopter and fly like a jet.

A modern-day builder re-created Fuller's Dymaxion car in 2011. He displayed it at a car show in Great Britain.

A MAN DRIVES A DYMAXION CAR AT AN EXHIBITION IN CHICAGO IN 1933. FULLER'S IDEA FOR A FLYING CAR NEVER GOT OFF THE GROUND.

In 1933 and 1935, Fuller built three prototypes of the Dymaxion car. One car crashed in Chicago. The other two passed from owner to owner. No car company ever mass-produced the vehicle. Fuller gave up on the car and focused on other inventions.

On the Fly

Fuller's Dymaxion car failed, but inventors have not given up on the flying car. More than twenty aircraft companies are building and testing flying cars. If they succeed, you might see flying cars in the sky in the 2020s.

Buckminister Fuller never made a flying car, but many modern companies are building them. This one is called the AeroMobil.

The Road to Failure

John DeLorean dreamed of building a futuristic sports car. In 1973, he formed the DeLorean Motor Company. The business built about nine thousand DeLoreans.

The cars had an eye-catching door design. Instead of swinging to the side as ordinary car doors do, DeLorean doors swung upward. When the doors were open, a DeLorean looked as if it had wings.

John DeLorean got in trouble with the law, and his business failed in 1982. But his car made an impact. In the 1985 movie *Back to the Future*, the main character uses a DeLorean as a time machine. In the twenty-first century, thousands of car lovers still drive, collect, and restore DeLoreans.

DeLorean sports cars

Try, Try, and Try Again

Making a successful invention is not easy. It requires skill and sometimes luck. Some inventions, such as synthetic dyes, come about by accident. Other inventions, such as Bubble Wrap and Post-it Notes, go nowhere at first but succeed later. Still other inventions, such as concrete houses and flying cars, might be the technology of the future. They all show that failure can be a step on the road to success.

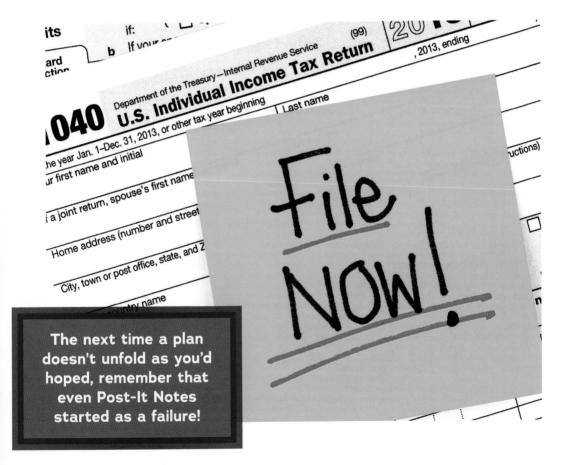

The next time a plan doesn't unfold as you'd hoped, remember that even Post-It Notes started as a failure!

Glossary

alcohol: a chemical mixture with many uses. Some kinds of alcohol dissolve dirt and grease.

coal tar: a black, sticky liquid that comes from coal

futuristic: having a high-tech, ultramodern design

malaria: a serious and sometimes deadly disease carried by mosquitoes

mass-produce: to manufacture in large quantities, usually using powerful machines

prototype: a full-size model of a car, airplane, or other machine, created before mass-production begins

synthetic: made by humans, usually by combining chemicals and other substances, instead of coming from nature

technology: the processes, methods, and tools used to carry out a task or build something

textured: having a rough, bumpy, or shaped surface instead of a flat surface

3D: short for three-dimensional. A 3D image looks as if it has depth instead of appearing flat.

3D printer: a machine that creates an object, such as a wall, by laying down row upon row of building material

Learn More about Invention Fails

Books

Farndon, John. *Inventions: A Visual Encyclopedia*. New York: DK, 2018. Read about world-changing inventions in the areas of transportation, communication, health care, space exploration, and more.

Kenney, Karen Latchana. *What Makes Vehicles Safer?* Minneapolis: Lerner Publications, 2016. Learn about antilock brakes, airbags, and other devices that help people travel safely.

Kenney, Karen Latchana. *Who Invented the Movie Camera? Edison vs. Friese-Greene*. Minneapolis: Lerner Publications, 2018. Both Thomas Edison and William Friese-Greene invented the movie camera around the same time. This book examines the race to be first in the movie business.

Websites

Inventive Kids
http://inventivekids.com/
This website introduces famous inventors and inventions and offers games and projects to help you learn more.

Kid Inventors' Day
http://www.kidinventorsday.com/
This website offers tips for kid inventors and provides links to books about inventions and contests for kid inventors.

National Geographic Kids: Cool Inventions
https://kids.nationalgeographic.com/explore/youtube-playlist-pages/youtube-playlist-cool-inventions/
This website includes articles and videos about inventors and inventions.

Index

Photo Acknowledgments

Image credits: schankz/Shutterstock.com, p. 4; apiwut sookkasame/Shutterstock.com, p. 5; sirtravelalot/Shutterstock.com, p. 6; ArnoldReinhold/Wikimedia Commons (CC BY-SA 3.0), p. 7; AP Photo/Christopher Barth, p. 8; U.S. Patent #1,255,517, p. 9; Everett Collection, Inc/Alamy Stock Photo, p. 10; Minnesota Historical Society, p. 11; Kris Ubach and Quim Roser/Cultura/Getty Images, p. 12; Signe Dons/Wikimedia Commons (public domain), p. 13; Maica/iStock/Getty Images, p. 14; gollykim/iStock/Getty Images, p. 15; Acroterion/Wikimedia Commons (CC BY-SA 4.0), p. 16; Library of Congress (LC-USZ62-78947), p. 17; Wellcome Library, London/Wikimedia Commons (CC BY 4.0), p. 18; Science & Society Picture Library/Getty Images, pp. 19, 22, 23; H. Krisp/Wikimedia Commons (CC BY 3.0), p. 20; Peter O'Connor/flickr (CC BY-SA 2.0), p. 21; Bettmann/Getty Images, p. 24; Sicnag/Wikimedia Commons (CC BY 2.0), p. 25; Arcaid Images/Alamy Stock Photo, p. 26; VALERY HACHE/AFP/Getty Images, p. 27; Paul Bersebach/Digital First Media/Orange County Register via Getty Images, p. 28; CatLane/iStock/Getty Images, p. 29.

Cover: Kevin Booth/Shutterstock.com.